Living with the Doors Wide Open

Living with the Doors Wide Open

Rebecca King Leet

Living with the Doors Wide Open
Copyright ©2018 Rebecca King Leet

ISBN: 978-1-940769-96-7
Publisher: Mercury HeartLink
Printed in the United States of America

All rights reserved. This book, or sections of this book, may not be reproduced or transmitted in any form without permission from the author, except for brief quotations embodied in articles, reviews, or used for scholarly purposes.

Permission is granted to educators to create copies of individual poems, with proper credits, for classroom or workshop assignments.

Contact the author at: *rebeccaleet@gmail.com*

Mercury HeartLink
www.heartlink.com

*Dedicated
to my daughters,
Caitlin and Kristin*

LIVING WITH THE DOORS WIDE OPEN

LIVING IN NATURE

Facing Your Sun	9
Out on a Limb, Alone	10
Learning to Fly	11
Morning News	12
Drinking Earl Grey Beneath a White Oak in Autumn	13
Squirrel Watching a Woman Drink Earl Grey Beneath a White Oak	14
Shading a Woman Drinking Earl Grey Beneath Me	15
Carolina Blue	16
Winter Scrum	17
Beyond the Canopy	18
No Birds in the Bog	20
Blue Jay Lyrics	21
Seeing the World for the First time	22
Autumn	23
Summer's Splendid Shroud	24
Green Gobblers	25
Musical Massage	26
The Zen of a Flounder	27
Another Incarnation	28
Sylvan Saloon	29
Buried Sound	30
Statue in the Shallows	31

LIVING IN FAMILY

The Iceman Leaveth	37
Abstract Art, Real Love	38
Most Peculiar Love	40
Migration	41
Dissolving Duet	42
Horn Concerto in E Flat Is Why	
I Want to Meet Mozart	43
Yellow Fur, Running Sore	44
One-Eyed Visitor	45
The Alchemy of Affection	46
First Love	47
Amber	48
Love in D Major	49
Hasty Words	50
Happiness Trap	51
Learning Early	52
Hydrangea	53
Mothering Backwards	54
Wobble and Creak	55
Gifting	56
Divorce Drums	58
What Is Seen	59
Myths Are Truths	60
Too Much Sand, Too Little Water	62
Knowing	64
Without Mother, Without Jane	65
No Moon in My Memory	66

A Corner of Heaven	68
'Tis But the Time	69
Chucking My Wedding Ring on a Highway	70
Livin' with the One I Love Blues	71

LIVING IN THE WORLD

Why History Repeats	75
What Feeds on Decay	76
Hidden in Plain Sight	77
The Temerity of Tulips	79
Unholy Happenings	80
Meeting Someone I Know in Manet's *The Plum*	82
Picasso's Pique	83
Someday May the Sash Sleep	84
Master of the Hunt	86
At What Point Do We Break	88

LIVING INSIDE

The Mist of Mystery	93
To an Artist Turning 18	95
Five Cents of Satisfaction	97
Passing Prayer	98
What's Inhaled	99
By a Stone Already Etched	100
Winter Solstice	101
The Destiny of Destiny	102
Ode to Late Bloomers	103
Stone Still on a Park Bench	104

Despair's Slender Strand	105
Is It Will to Live	106
Gold Leaf and Letting Go	107
Hidden in the Ivy	108
Meadow Pond	109
The Redbud	110
Visitation in Leaf Clothing	112
Toyotas and Transfiguration	113
Falling	114
Now Certain	115
Ebb Tide	116
Acknowledgements and Thanks	119
About the Author	121

I sent my Soul through the Invisible,
Some letter of that After-Life to spell:
And by and by my Soul return'd to me,
And answer'd "I Myself am Heav'n and Hell."

Omar Khayyam
The Rubaiyat

Living in Nature

Facing Your Sun

As the fence turns downhill,
pickets merge – a façade
of white wall cordoning off
life outside from life within.

Here, where pickets stand
solitary posts, a green tendril
snakes between twin guards,
offering escape to a single rose.

I pause to inhale its sweetness
and see specks of dark red in the crimson
– a few petals toward autumn,
it is still a magnificent bloom.

Over the pickets, I see comrades wilted
and wan. *Stay facing the sun that warms you,*
I whisper, *it has kept you open
past the season others knew.*

Out on a Limb, Alone

He perches on the pine's low branch, staring
in the dining room window, exuding the same uncertainty
as when he tarried on the patio fence this morning

while I sat out drinking tea. His neck retracts turtlishly.
His shoulders hunch. He looks aimlessly right then left
without any sign he expects to find what he seeks –

or certainty he knows what that is. It's a universal mien,
not species specific – a postural pronouncement
of home recently left, the need to find one's way,

the fear of being unready. I remember it from my youth
and feel it again at this other end of life, in a new house.
A thin speckled chest bespeaks his age as clearly

as white hair does mine. Soon his chest will round
and feathers turn red-orange; the moment we've shared
will take wing.

Learning to Fly

Baby sparrows get confused, end up
hanging on the window screen,
but young mourning doves
keep deep inside the white pine

where bare limbs provide an open practice field.
Little doves dawdle, doubt, flit up
one branch, take a breather, hop back down,
pace, waffle. Then it's flaps up again.

They're building muscle for forays yet unknown,
as I did on the jungle gym at Lomond Elementary.
Steel bars stacked in squares six feet high –
I could only reach the next one if I let go and stretched.

Morning News

On the patio, the chaise sags at the back with my impression and most of the rest with yours. The sports page of *The Washington Post* hangs like a lap-robe over my bent knees, sliding me into the worrisome world via more incidental fare: Serena Williams may capture tennis' Grand Slam in four more matchless matches. The air is two ounces lighter in lassitude, the white oak two leaves lighter on the limb.

I sip English Breakfast and watch the edges of your rubber nose twitch as though victimized by a ceaseless tickle. Your bronze muzzle lifts and turns periscope-slow to the right, then the left. Sphagnum-soft ears tack back, relax forward. We're both learning what happened in the world while we slept.

Drinking Earl Grey Beneath a White Oak in Autumn

There's a rowdy brunch in my oak tree this morning.
Eight or nine guests at table – hard to count precisely
because they shift constantly, like children
playing musical chairs. They're a noisy group:

nonstop chatter, screeches and fulmination.
And excessively messy: my patio is covered with shell detritus
like what you find under seats in a baseball stadium.
Despite the threat of acorn bombs, I bring my tea out

and settle onto the chaise with my Sunday paper.
I finish the front section before a shell shard
lands in my cup. It's small price to pay. Winter
will soon come; I'm glad my company has

this all-you-can-eat opportunity. One of the diners
takes a break, comes to sit on the fence and look at me.
I look back. We're like strangers who smile as they pass
on a walk – alive together, aware of each other.

Squirrel Watching a Woman Drink Earl Grey Beneath a White Oak

Now here is someone who knows how
to spend Sunday morning. I regret
my earlier intrusion; interlopers

jangled my nerves. Each year, my home
is their first stop on the harvest tour,
binging here on sweet nuts before moving

to less savory ones on the red oak next door.
They lack manners: they race, rassle, shriek,
squabble. Periodic evacuation is essential.

Sitting on this fence, I feel like an escapee
from an asylum; she seems not to care, serenely
sipping tea. Surely, she forgives the shell I dropped.

Shading a Woman Drinking Earl Grey Beneath Me

Ah, she's back to lingering over tea, luxuriating in my shade
while I'm still leafed out. My homies look happy: she's poured
a second cup and the squirrels seem to have invited
all their friends. Everyone loves me in fall – it's my favorite time.
I mostly rest all winter. Spring brings lots of work
pushing out twigs, catkins, leaves. Summer is stressful –
I need to reach deep during dry spells, hold tight in storms.
Autumn is party-time. Being a white oak in autumn...
what could be better?

Carolina Blue

Dawn rolls herself upward
in bands of confederate gray
and Carolina blue
regular as mattress ticking
on an old double bed,
painting the winter sky
with ambivalence.

Winter Scrum

Huddle of overinflated footballs
statue-still
in a slice of severed floe:
thermodynamics,
mallard-style.

Beyond the Canopy

Now that I know trees are,
in many ways, like us – sharing,
asking for help, acting communally –
it feels like family when I walk
through these familiar woods.

An imposing oak at the trailhead
no longer fades into faceless forest
but comes forth as a *mother tree*
feeding saplings beneath its boughs –
some spawned from acorns it bore.

Further on, a supine maple,
in slow decay, redeems virtue
as a *nurse tree*. Woody seedlings
and small plants sprout from
the fecundity of its moldering middle.

A regal beech tempts me to tarry
and admire its gold umbrella sheltering
a cluster of young trees. Too much sun
might make them grow tall before
they grow strong. Which, I wonder,

will ever know full sun? For trees –
as for people – greatest growth comes
where the canopy cleaves. Yet, those who
pierce it – seemingly triumphant –
find themselves in a new and isolated

existence. Gone are the comfort
and camaraderie of the second story.
In trade: the thrill and throe of discovery,
the ecstasy of Creation – yet loneliness
of few to share it with.

My walk ends at the river, where I rest
my tired body against a kindred
companion: a lone sycamore, slowly
shedding parchment.

No Birds in the Bog

Not yet midwinter, a grim sky
shrouds desolate treetops. Ice
melts soil to sludge. The human heart
beats as in a bog. Not so

the heart of a downy woodpecker,
whose staccato drilling breaks the silence
as she hunts for breakfast. Or
the lone blue jay who – lustfully –

whistles for company, his indigo body stark
against white sycamore bark. Or a flamboyant
male cardinal trilling *prettee* as he surveys
mallards fishing in the frigid creek.

Blue Jay Lyrics

Its landing bows the white oak branch
like a five-year-old's bottom indents a trampoline,
and from my chair on the patio

I see a flash of tongue-shaped blue tail
and all the white underside. It hops sideways
and emits a signature squawk that evokes

a grumpy old geezer shaking his fist
at young boys riding bikes across his lawn.
The blue jay hops again and again,

each time piercing the morning peace:
bounce-squawk, bounce-squawk,
bounce-squawk. I picture the bouncing ball

that springs word-to-word
over lyrics projected on a mammoth screen
in a Baptist megachurch.

Seeing the World for the First Time

Spring birdsong is a halleluiah chorus:
the tenor *prettee-prettee* of the cardinal
and mezzo response of his partner,
sweet whistle and trill of song sparrows,
soulful coos of mourning doves. They sing
joyous proclamation that winter is past,
the world has come alive again. Then –

do you notice – quiet descends after all that
melodious courting and nest-building.
Only a stray note here and there
as parents birth and feed their young.

Come summer, new voices intone. At first,
just chips of sound and sharp yeeps – quiet,
quivering – but soon overwritten
by soprano solos with rapturous refrains.

Autumn

Red, yellow, brown mittens
   slip-
       sliding
on fall currents,
waving goodbye
to summer.

Summer's Splendid Shroud

The crepe myrtle's last
      raspberry blossoms
            kiss their branches goodbye
                  and feather the grave
                        of summer.

Green Gobblers

More and more sprout each day,
unfurling
to start feeding the elm.
The green mouths –
always open –
hang from every branch
and twig,
carbo-loading sun up to sun down.
Quiet, contained, undemanding –
none asks for more
than the sun provides.

Come fall,
when the feast is finished,
I'll rake
their tired brown bodies
into piles
and await next year's
leafy multitude.

Musical Massage

Low, sweet coos of mourning doves.
Staccato voices of children at play.
Warm winds slipping between new leaves.

I give myself to these melodies
and the long fingers of their massage
play down my spine like a keyboard,
releasing me from winter.

The Zen of a Flounder

Water at the east end of Grand Cayman
more often rolls than roils, but today
it is flat as day-old coke at the beach bar.
A shimmer of turquoise when viewed from shore,

the beauty goes unnoticed by snorkelers
spread-eagle and face down on its surface,
heads swinging back and forth like metronomes
as we feverishly pursue surprise. Fierce morning sun

beams diamond clarity into the underworld;
only a sinking Bud Lite can taints the tableau.
Two squid morph from light brown to colorless
as swimmers near; a barracuda gently fishtails

over green sea grass. Suddenly, the ocean floor
moves under me. A flat disc big as a dinner plate
lifts off, skimming the bottom as faint flutters
propel it forward. Royal blue circles freckle the body,

two eyes pop up at its front like tiny periscopes.
I inhale to dive and snap a picture, but its languid movement
causes pause. I exhale, tuck my camera and float,
bowing to the Zen of the peacock flounder.

Another Incarnation

How hits the sun that these few leaves,
sturdy on the bone-white sycamore branch,
are clothed in autumn hues –

red and rust and paling yellow harbingers
of life's transition – while their sisters
still drape summer's green full force?

Do the leaves sense their election?
Does that knowledge starch aging spines,
excite them as scouts of another incarnation –

or yoke them with foretaste of death
and incline them toward a future
made brittle by desperate holding on?

The same rays find my head, turning
the gold-red locks of my summertime
into white-gold herald of a future mine to ordain.

Sylvan Saloon

Honeysuckle weaves in
            and out of the wire fence
like dancers – freeze-framed –
            at a Saturday night hoedown.
Each fluted flower brims
            with hummingbird whiskey.
An emerald-hatted wrangler
            bellies up to the bar
and hovers, reckoning the line
            of shot glasses.
He shoots his straw – deadeye –
            into the first,
sucks brusquely, repeats down the line.
            He swigs
the last jigger and exits the saloon,
            weaving slightly.

Buried Sound

What does a great gray owl hear
when a mouse burrows two feet

under Arctic snow? Sound like a skater
scraping ice, or the dull grind

of a garden auger? Does noise echo
as though reverberating

off culvert walls? If I could invade
the sanctum of others' buried thoughts,

what vibrations might I hear. Would
a lover's unspoken anger crackle

like distant lightening, a friend's private judgment
groan like an old door closing?

Statue in the Shallows

Odd. Just plain odd. No other word for it.
It's hard to see, against the backdrop
of beech and brush at the edge of the river.
Fisherfolk stare across the water – pondering

why a statue would be planted in such a spot.
Two reedy posts for a base, a torso in the mold
of a bloated football, the top an L-shaped pole,
tilted. Odd spot for artwork – waterfowl

are the area's main visitors. Mallards fly low,
leapfrogging each other. An osprey jets down,
hooks a fish, leaves. Every 30 seconds, a cormorant
slides feet-first to a watery landing, like

a baseball player trying to beat the tag at third.
Sounds are few, faint: plop of a lure breaking
the dull green surface, soft rhythm of paddles
as kayakers mosey downstream. In two bends

they'll spy the iconic Washington Monument.
The only other urban inkling, now and then,
is a silver Boeing 757 lumbering toward a landing –
like the cormorant, feet-first. The statue is miniature

compared to bronze equestrians who inhabit
parks and traffic circles across the city – curiously
including Joan of Arc. Someone with a strong arm –
and stronger conceit – might hurl a rock across the Potomac

at the statue; it would fall short. That thought
flies away as frawk, frawk breaks the stillness,
the statue sprouts colossal wings and, graceful
as a ballerina, the great blue heron lifts skyward.

Living in Family

The Iceman Leaveth

Ice transmutes
as forces beyond its control
decide the future. My father

knows the same fate.
He disappears slowly,
like ice on a farmer's pond –

every day a little more lost
though I can't identify
exactly where.

Abstract Art, Real Love

You almost never found me, in that gallery
off Piazza San Marco. You got off the train
one stop too soon, remember? At Venice-Mestre
not Venice. You and your mother pushed through

the station door, saw no canal, realized the error.
A nearby woman, in rolled up blue jeans,
turned and asked, in flat midwestern voice,
are you looking for Venus too? For 30 years,

you two laughed over that story, until the day
her brow creased in confusion and she began
to slip away. The trip, a 60th birthday present,
fulfilled her lifelong desire. Though not one

to journal, she wrote daily: Prague viewed from
the Ambassador's car, US flags on the bumper;
Vienna's musical vibration; a posh Paris restaurant
where she ordered rabbit and was first presented

with the raw skinned body on a silver tray
surrounded by white carnations. And the Venice art gallery.
You both admired an abstract sculpture – 56 pounds
of solid, soft gray glass. It cost $800, a bank-busting

sum on your salary. But you bought it. Friends
shook their heads, doubting the sculpture would arrive
in one piece. Three months later, it did – I did,
all 56 pounds of my soft gray glass. Ever since,

I have resided on this pedestal in your living room.
Few guests remark on me, though one said I look
like big Pac-man eating little Pac-man. He missed
what you both saw: a mother nestling a child on her lap.

Most Peculiar Love

When a bluebird fledge takes wing,
is a slice of her mother's heart
caught between sleek feathers?

When a lion coursing with youth
leaves his mother's pride, does sorrow
muffle her roar?

As you embark to claim destiny
half a world away, with you goes
a piece of my wilting heart.

Love of a child you bore and bred
is the strangest of loves: the reward
for loving with relentless abandon –

hoping every morning, praying every night
and trying every moment in between –
is that if your dreams come true,

one day you stand on your front step
and watch your love
depart.

Migration

Peppers sizzle in the fry-pan,
a red-yellow-orange celebration of summer;
      pubescent daughters banter, semi-heard.

Warm breezes slip through the screen
feathering cheeks with the last kiss of the season;
      a woman-child brushes my back, moves on.

Far away, geese in migration sound signal
of the season's passing, a warning to savor –
more than sweet peppers and summer's caress –
      moments of a season never to return.

Dissolving Duet

A familiar polonaise plays
on the Bose my brother bought;
it sits by a wide window overlooking

nothing notable. In empty space,
I again see fingers move flawlessly
across ebony and ivory, fingers

now leaden in my mother's lap.
Notes once inexorably etched
in mind and muscle have evaporated

as though scored in disappearing ink.
Only one name will be carved
on the tombstone, but the pianist

will not pass away alone. Chopin plays on
as I mourn the mother fading to black
and the little girl beside her on the bench.

Horn Concerto in E Flat Is Why I Want to Meet Mozart

I want to meet Mozart and thank him
for music that pinioned love for my father
in the years my ears were stopped.

Daddy played French horn like a man
making love. Before gin stole his soul –
and robbed me –

he was transformed when that brass beauty
nestled on his lap, his lips settled
on its mouth, hand rested in the bell.

His cheeks would balloon, then expel notes
soft as warm honey or fluttering
fast as hummingbird wings. During the war

he played in a Navy band, reckoned
it was no way to fight, and transferred
to ships in the Pacific. Once home,

fatherhood scuttled hopes of reentering
college to become a teacher; he sold
insurance instead.

If music predates speech, then love dwells
not in the realm of cognition –
where it may be dissected and expelled –

but in the more impregnable limbic land
where it plays pianissimo, till resounding
at the first notes of Mozart.

Yellow Fur, Running Sore

I buried Buddy today. A worm turned.

I lifted the dusty box off my shelf,
rescued a spade from honeysuckle,
picked a spot under the spring-splendid

redbud, and dug. Chunks of loam ceded
to Virginia soil. I shoveled, then scraped
black humus and red clay with bare hands

to make a bed. I nestled Buddy in
and gently coaxed the earth up and over,
crumbling clumps into clods then bits,

softening his forever rest. Tears came –
welling up, dribbling down, wetting his grave
as I crumbled the dirt ever smaller and
ever smaller and ever smaller and smoothed

and smoothed until my smoothing became
caressing – and I petted the soil as though
touching his yellow fur and the running sore

of decayed love that was life when he trotted
into it. I sat on my knees, hands stilled,
and watched nature's transformative agents

begin. I surrendered the past to worms.

One-Eyed Visitor

There is little wood for the fire, little food
in the cupboard, the candle is burning low when
there comes a scratch at the door. The cold
makes us hesitate before opening. When we do,
we first see a small shivering body, then fright
in baleful brown eyes so characteristic of a pug.
One eye assesses us through milky film. The other
is forever shut, pointing to a pirate's life. Ribs show
through sagging fur, here or there an ice crystal
lodges in his blond coat. Snow has sequestered us
for two days; we wonder how long he's suffered.
There is little wood for the fire, little food
in the cupboard, and the candle's burnt low
when we invite him in.

The Alchemy of Affection

As always when she tells a tale,
her whole body surges toward me
like a warm wave about to crash.
Chardonnay wafts on her words;

her front teeth jut. Rills of wrinkles
run south from her eyes, north
from her lips. One hand rises
as if to absorb the explosion of delight

provoked yet again. Laughter snaps
my head back, hunches my shoulders.
The camera captures red hair
shading ginger on my head, ash blonde

fading white on hers; we're women
of an age that adds mystery
to the alchemy of affection: how
the love of deep friendship transmutes

into the friendship of deep love.
Between us, three failed marriages.
Before us, the chance yet to claim
passion puzzling as it is fervent.

First Love

The hound's head dropped,
his sleek, muscled body slid
into a slink. Left paws inched
forward, then right ones, stalking
the summer-plump squirrel.
In scoring range, the hound paused;
pursuer and pursued locked eyes.
With a twitch, the squirrel shot up
a white oak, glared down
at the tedious canine howling
below. I thought of Jack: how
I'd hungered, hesitated. And lost.

Amber

Passion that imprints
with hydraulic force –
a baby's birth,
lover's betrayal,
stranger's assault –
outlasting breath that fuels a moment
destined to disappear
when the flickering ordinariness of life flares,
this beetle in resin
which poetry transforms
into amber.

Love in D Major

I wish, all these years later, we had not buried
my father's French horn with him. He died
piece by piece over years. The space where his left leg
would have been made room for the horn
in his casket. Had I the horn, it would grace

my living room wall, a sinuous sculpture
ready to resound once more. *Quiet,*
Daddy would command in the middle of dinner,
always accompanied by Mozart, Strauss
or Bach. *Listen to that French horn*!

He often played the Mozart concerto
I heard in church today. At the first notes
I saw him again, nestled in the curve
of the grand piano that dominated our living room.
Mama was a pianist and they often played together,

creating a love sound even a child heard.
Over troubled years, they curved into each other
less and less. Then the music stopped. Not long ago,
I found a French horn ornament, brought it out
at Christmas, and heard my father whole again.

Hasty Words

How like a rosebud fallen is my heart
when the skies of May dawn ashen
and your face is turned from me.

What would bloom scarlet
across a thousand tomorrows
lies forsaken, a hint of color promised

fading to the pale of yesterday.

Happiness Trap

Mary Sunshine, Mary Sunshine

Eyes so bright,
hug so tight.

Mary Sunshine, Mary Sunshine

Always clowning,
never frowning.

Mary Sunshine, Mary Sunshine

Smile that twinkles,
nose that crinkles.

Mary Sunshine, Mary Sunshine

Always caring,
ne'er despairing.

Mary Sunshine, Mary Sunshine

Not a peep,
just a leap
        right
        off
        the
        roof.

Learning Early

The body has no head –

a taupe-colored mound, softball size,
plopped next to my neighbor's SUV.
Pointing toward me, as I approach

with sad trepidation, is a tail too new
to be fully bushed, lying flat, still as death.
As I draw close, a small head pops up

from the far end, swinging left and right
in sleepy rhythm. Shoo, I say, waving my arms
and stepping closer. Half-heartedly,

the baby squirrel ambles five feet away, stops,
looks back. Go, I scold, *you have to learn
what to fear.* My words quick-freeze in air

and I am once more the little girl
who had to learn early what to fear.

Hydrangea

Each July, lacy buttermilk blossoms
big as melons
cover Nana's hydrangea.
It is very large.
I am very small.

It has a hollow inside,
like some big bushes do,
where a child can hide.
It's shady,
damp ground chills bare toes.

I feel safe from all the world there –
protected, and embraced like in the arms
of a big-bosomed mama.
This garden is ever in bloom
the dirt always cool, and I am forever
a little girl who feels safe.

Mothering Backwards

I'm sorry, she says, what
are your daughters' names?
Those, twenty-five and twenty-six,
for whom she'd drawn down
Social Security each month

to ensure they'd go to college. Whose
University of Virginia sweatshirt
and William and Mary tee she'd worn
proudly. She'd sit stone still, listening
to each story Caitlin and Kristin shared.

*I don't remember – what
are your daughters' names?*
asks the woman who was my mother
of the woman who is her mother now.

Wobble and Creak

Like a 19th century steamer trunk,
you've carried what I needed
to navigate the seas of life with rare freedom:

from the constraint of gender,
the inconvenience of invisibility,
the bondage of others' definitions.

Now your joints wobble and creak,
your sinews dry and crack.
Your skeleton bows wearily, contoured

by tennis championships too numerous
to evoke and wilderness adventures
too perilously engaged.

Ah, my dear, you've grown old,
acquired a sepia sheen.

How ungrateful my anger.
How absurd my resentment.
How foolish my surprise.

Gifting

My grandmother took me to the movies only once.
It was *The Ten Commandments* and she hoped
to imprint Biblical lessons on my seven-year-old heart.

But what seared into memory was a scene of slaves –
whipped by overseers – using leather straps to drag
limestone massives into place, building a pyramid.

The lash of conscience drives me to visit my mother
on her 94th birthday, dragging a heart pyramid-heavy.
My wish is she never see her 95th. She lies abed, as usual,

breathing lightly, corpse-still. Maybe sleeping, maybe not.
White hair marbled with silver splays on the pillow;
raw, dull marble, not polished. Her face, so oddly

unwrinkled, wears a premature death mask.
Her mouth gapes. I squeeze next to her on the bed
but her body doesn't respond to my presence

nor her cold hand to my squeeze. Is this chill
what an undertaker feels? Different from mitten-less hands
in winter, but impossible to say quite how. I lay my hand

along her cheek, dry as old paper in the attic;
the creases next to her closed eyes flinch.
At least I tell myself they do.

There is little bulk to her body except her belly;
it looks like all her insides slid down into a bloat there.
I stare at my first home, thinking of her body holding me,

gifting me with life. Now I hold her with my body,
wishing I could return the gift
...with death.

Divorce Drums

I never donned fatigues, hunkered down in trenches,
or marched to fife and drum. But perhaps I know
how it feels before any great battle:

eerie quiet. All has been spoken. Words
of anger and intimidation. Followed by
compromise and conciliation. None can stave it off.

In the quiet comes calm, callous and cold. Gone
is the fuel that ignited passion, sustained mock battles.
And flowed like lava during skirmishes.

In the calm comes sadness, abysmal and abiding.
Indignation, rage, murderous desire to drain
the last drop from a severed jugular – all gone.

In the sadness comes knowing. Even those
who've never heard a trumpet charge sense
there are no victors in a great battle. All who engage

lose. Whether combatant or not, those who do not die
are maimed. Who are not crippled are scarred. None
leaves the field without suffering.

Shells bite deepest in a civil war. When all the victims
once dined at the same table, slept under the same roof,
dreamt the same dreams, the anguish defies description.

Yet knowing is not joined by surrender. The cause for which
the battle is fought still lives. Those who flee battles
in which history places them, bequeath them to their children.

What Is Seen

I'll tell you what
    my eyes see
and you tell me
    about yours
and together we may see
    what is true

Myths Are Truths

I can tell you the reason, but you won't really know
'til you cradle your baby in the deepness of night
and wonder...how can I teach this child
all she needs to learn?

By herself, she'll discover
that heat can hurt,
dawn means a new day,
snowflakes melt.

From others, she'll learn
that c-a-t is that furry lump,
two plus two equals four,
periods end sentences.

From me she'll need transcendent lessons:
of accepting love,
of receiving gifts from One unseen,
of being blessed just for being.

One way I'll teach her is by telling a myth
many times over many years. Later,
she will think it a lie but it's not.
Myths are truths you know best with your heart.

The myth passed to me from my parents
and to them from theirs, on down for generations.
She will teach it to her children
so they can learn.

This myth, like most, once had a truth you could touch.
There was a man – a gentle and generous soul –
who loved children just because they were children
and gifted them just to give them joy.

His body lived and died centuries ago,
but his spirit lives and is made flesh
every Christmas by parents who learned as children
that Santa Claus brings more than candy and toys -

> he brings an expectation of goodness and grace
> that endures as long as you believe.

Too Much Sand, Too Little Water

Silence tastes like honey
in the early years
our be-with-you-ness
as we sit at each end of the couch
extending our legs toward each other
you knitting me reading
and from time to time I'll read you a passage
and you'll still the music of your needles
nod appreciatively and radiate love
and sometimes you'll turn your foot sideways
run the socked sole up and down my thigh
and I'll smile love back.

The green-purple lamp we bought –
because the glaze stunned us –
dusts the air with golden particles.

In later years, we sit upright at each end
of the couch, front-facing. Your knitting
has less melody; I share fewer passages;
you cannot reach my thigh with your sole.
Silence has no flavor.

The lamp's finish has crazed into a spider web
and its glow surrendered to cool white.

Near the end, I read on one couch.
You knit on the other. Your needles clack harshly,
as though angry at the wool.
There are no passages I brave to tender.
The feel of your sole is a memory.

The lamp has cracked. Maybe the original clay
had too much sand, too little water, been fired
too hot, too long. Maybe it simply succumbed
to the weariness of clay drained of elasticity.

It no longer burns.

Knowing

You knew before
the dogwood bloomed
this was our last summer.

You stayed.

At a place of unknown
knowing, I felt our fate
and packed my heart away.

Without Mother, Without Jane

> She stared silent goodbyes/
> ...and her eyes stuck open.
> —Donald Hall, *Without*

In the waning weeks, mother's eyes stayed shut in a way
not like sleep but a corpse breathing; I might have been
in a museum, talking to a reclining bronze. The last night,
as words lodged like dry bread in my throat, her eyes
stared straight ahead – stuck open, just as Donald Hall
described Jane Kenyon on their final day. I wonder if he too
closed her lids at the end, grateful for this one last gift.

No Moon in My Memory

Milwaukee, deep winter many, many
years ago. My six-year-old brother runs
and slides on the ice-covered driveway
abutting our house. On three-year-old legs
I try fruitlessly to keep up.

He falls.

In later telling, Daddy said he'd warned us
to slide sideways, not straight ahead
so we wouldn't hit our heads if we fell.

A little boy forgot.

Where does a child lodge remembrance
in the years before she knows words
for what is seen and heard? Is there
a little drawer in the far brain which,
with the slightest jiggle a lifetime later,
can pop open and unsought understanding
float out like a ghost?

I don't remember seeing my brother fall
or seeing him spread out on the ice.
But I see the pool of blood under his head
and hear my father's angry voice. Years later,
he told me Daddy was yelling *Stop crying! Get up!*
Daddy was always afraid I'd be weak, he said.

Yesterday a friend recounted a story about
her first childhood memory: she described
sitting on her father's shoulders, wondering together
at the moon. A drawer popped open,

a cold breeze ruffled the air.

A Corner of Heaven

To fashion a space where a child feels safe
is to create a corner of heaven.

To listen with ears that sense hurts not revealed
is to hear with the heart of an angel.

To hold out a hand that a child will grasp
is to proffer the fingers of God.

'Tis But the Time

> That we shall die we know;
> 'tis but the time
> —Shakespeare

Waiting to cross the six-lane, mind floating
free as falling petals – till jolted by screeching
tires. I'd have known only in the last seconds.
The spinning car found traction, completed its turn
just shy of my toes, left me still staring: *Don't Walk*.

Eight years ago, Honduras, 2 a.m., a seaside hotel
on skimpy stilts. I wouldn't have known at all –
not seen the flash offshore, learned the earthquake
registered 7.3. Tectonic plates shifted sideways
instead of up: no tsunami.

Forty-seven years ago, the family dinner table.
My martini-fueled father flayed me with words
so vicious even my steeled psyche melted,
then stomped upstairs where he kept his gun.
I thought I knew, then. He grabbed car keys instead
and tore into the night.

Chucking My Wedding Ring on a Highway

We started out
in side-by-side lanes,
we thought –
at least I thought –
one day the lanes would merge
to one.

Now, I don't know
what you thought,
but it's been 11 years
and we're still in the same lanes.

I'm turning
on the next
exit ramp.

Livin' with the One I Love Blues

Seems I been livin' all my days
Seems I been livin' all my days
I surely been livin' all my days
With anger in the one I love.

Daddy was a drinkin' man
Proud man, lost his job, lost the next
Proud man gotta have a job
Or there be anger in his love.

Husband was a bully boy,
Fear-full, punchin' ghosts all day long
Fearful man never feels safe
So there be anger in his love.

Lover was a jealous one,
Wanna ban my chil'n, make 'em leave
Ain't no mama gonna make that choice
So there be anger in her love.

All my days, anger in the one I love.
All my days, but not no more,
I'm alone – livin' with the one, livin' with the one
Livin' with the one I love.

Living in the World

Why History Repeats

It's the sounds, the sounds
that replay vividly in memory – the crunch
of Ron's Army boots on the gravel path,
                whisper of anguished voices
                alive on the wind.
Left and right, we pass the outline of barracks,
holding pens for death at Dachau.

It's Viktor Frankl's urgent voice
as he leans close to describe losing his wife,
his parents, his entire family in the camps.

In my copy of <u>Man's Search for Meaning</u>
he writes:
                I wish my answers
            were as good as your questions.

It's the deafness of her heart –
the blond American mother eyeing the inscription
on a memorial where the gravel path turns:
                to honor the dead,
                to admonish the living.
Pivoting to go, she beckons her two sons
with an arm wave and calls with chirpy uplift:
                com'on kids,
            let's go to the ovens.

What Feeds on Decay

> Some are guilty, but all are responsible.
> —Rabbi Abraham Joshua Heschel

My last semester in college I lived in a house whose
Old South charm had long since gone with the wind:
leaky roof, collapsing front porch, walls so copiously cracked
they presented as wallpaper with giant spiderweb motif.
We mostly ignored our co-tenants – cockroaches.

Few ventured out in the light of day. They emerged
in the dark; flipping on a bathroom light in the middle of the night
sent multitudes skittering. We tolerated the vermin – soon
they'd be someone else's problem. The violence in Charlottesville
reminded me of our roach resignation. Americans have accepted

an infestation of human roaches: Nazis and white supremacists.
We've known they exist in dank sewers, feed on our decay, emerge
occasionally. We wanted to believe they were few. But the light
turned on in Charlottesville, incinerating denial. Our home is teeming
and that triggers the question: are they the problem – or are we?

In 2017, white supremacists and Nazis held a rally in Charlottesville, VA that touched off violent confrontations with counter-demonstrators. A woman was killed and many people injured when a white supremacist drove a car into counter-demonstrators.

Hidden in Plain Sight

> Sewall- Belmont House
> Home of the National Women's Party

Relentlessly seen and relentlessly hidden –
like the Muslim maiden in an aubergine niqab –

every move is scrutinized by self-appointed purists
prowling their small world trolling for errors of orthodoxy,

the license needed to flay her for sins of omission
or commission – Hillary Clinton is hidden in plain sight.

Every hair style scanned, every outfit evaluated,
every gesture the object of doubt and every word sifted

through a sieve so fine no Biblical prophet could pass muster –
she, like her niqab-clad sister, reveals herself only in her eyes,

the element most resistant to programmed posturing.
Often enough, they are opaque panes – double-frosted

to protect against those who would pierce her chain mail
for sport or spite. When she first campaigned for president,

I caught her alone briefly as we crossed paths leaving an event
at the Sewall-Belmont House and saw the window shades

fail fleetingly and pain-stained eyes soften in gratitude
when I simply said, *thank you for running.*

Sen. Hillary Clinton campaigned in 2008 to be the Democratic Party nominee for President. She failed in 2008 but won the nomination in 2016.

The Temerity of Tulips

> after *A Song in the Front Yard*
> by Gwendolyn Brooks

In a town so small it pinched,
Martha Sue longed to be a bit naughty –
a lot naughty not being an option
for a girl stuck in a world so black and white
that showing red got censored as sin.
Rebellious yet sensibly sly,
and sick of self-appointed saints,
she planted row after row of scarlet bulbs
in the gardens of dowager crones – mute mutiny
she watched bloom into a triumph of tulips.

Unholy Happenings

I wonder what happened to Martha Sue Morrow
from Crawfordville, Georgia, who –
to get from home to college in Athens –

would stand at the town's only stoplight
and flag down the Trailways bus.
She returned from Thanksgiving

our freshman year and told me her mother
had helped her unpack her suitcase, snapping up
a pair of Martha Sue's panties, clutching them

to her breast with both hands and sighing
oh, cotton panties – you're still a good girl!—
nylon panties being clear proof of unholy happenings.

Martha Sue thought Athens, Georgia
was a wonderful place: it had a movie theater,
a restaurant that served hot dogs topped

with chili, and an actual station from which
buses came and went on a schedule. I thought
Athens was not such a wonderful place:

it had one movie theatre, cuisine was hot dogs
topped with chili, and there was no way
to get anywhere except by bus. I grew up

where there were stoplights, a house where
the President lived, theaters that offered live
performances plus many that showed movies,

and to get most places worth going to, you flew.
I once told Martha Sue about being held out of school
one day to go downtown and watch a funeral cortege

take President Kennedy's body to lie in state
at the Capitol. I wonder if Martha Sue ever wonders
what happened to me.

Meeting Someone I Know in Manet's *The Plum*

The eyes, barren and black,
capture mine as I cross
the marble threshold. I jerk away,

seeking softness with Cassatt
and Morisot. But her stare haunts;
I succumb to the unease at being watched

and lock eyes with a tinctured soul
hibernating from self. We both look past
the plum marinating in a dish, corn-straw hair

escaping her hat. A sense of having met
hovers over me as I slip on my wool coat
and enter the desolate medium of winter.

Picasso's Pique

An art historian would blanch
to hear my memory
has misplaced which titan it was –
neurons whisper *Picasso*.

No matter; the point is, on the wall
preceding the treasure were a half-dozen
half-drawn sketches: fumbled forays.
Those I remember.

Warped fingers, oversized palms, convoluted
wrists. Try, fail, try again, fail again;
you could almost hear him mutter
oh, mierda over and over. How heartened

I was by the hurdles that tripped the master.
Hope fluttered inside like little butterfly wings.
There might be more artists if museums
dedicated as much space to struggle as to success.

Someday May the Sash Sleep

> I have often to remark the fortitude
> with which women sustain the most
> overwhelming reverses of fortune.
> —Washington Irving

The sash, gold with purple letters,
remarkably untattered almost 40 years
after draping my chest for a march

at the convention that nominated
Ronald Reagan. It was an artifact
when retrieved two months ago

from a cardboard trunk in the attic;
today it breathes anew, a satin Rip Van Winkle.
Fantasy is now reality. Donald Trump

is President. Women take to the streets
again. Pinning it on sends me immediately
back to a Detroit hotel room sweaty with bodies

crammed hip-to-hip watching bellied men
and bouffant women eliminate – after decades
of endorsement – the Equal Rights Amendment

from the platform Reagan would champion.
The daughter who now pins the sash on my shoulder
is the same age I was in Detroit. On Election Night,

we watched returns with others who marched there;
I'd brought the sash in anticipation of celebrating
at last. But as the returns began painting a picture

of our future with a misogynist leader,
she whispered *I didn't think this could happen.*
A century ago, 5,000 suffragettes – disenfranchised

denizens – marched down Pennsylvania Avenue
just before Woodrow Wilson took office. Now,
the morning after Trump's inauguration, my daughter

and I join a half-million overflowing ceremonial streets
joined by millions protesting across the globe.
Someday, oh please, someday, may the sash sleep.

The day after the inauguration of President Donald Trump, the Women's March on Washington *drew a half-million people demonstrating against him. More than 600 similar protests were held worldwide.*

Master of the Hunt

Amelia, you will not believe mah experience at the Washington Star when Ah took in Mr. Sands' obituary today.

First, Ah couldn't jes leave it at the dawr with the man. Ah had to take it up in this filthy elevatah to the newsroom.

You wouldn't believe the sight of that room – bigger than a ba'n and dirtier than mine or yours.

A young woman asted if Ah wanted to sit down. Lordee, Ah certainly did not. Ah was wearing mah mink!

Ah had everythin' written right there on the papah. But this young woman – Ah swear they have chil'in writin' the papah these days – she wants more information.

Ah said, mah dear, what questions could you hayve? Thomas Jefferson Sands III. 87. Died at home. Master of the Middleburg Foxhunt for 25 years. Ever since his daddy died.

Ah explained Mr. Sands jus' collapsed from a heart attack at Green Pastures. And that his mayn Big Jimmy found him in the librar'. On the flowa.

Ah pointed out Ah'd listed who his people are, too.

Well, she said…you are not goin' to believe what she asted, Amelia… *what did he do*, she asted. Of course, Ah had no idea what she meant.

What did he do, she said again, *what was his job?* Mah jaw dropped.

Ah did not know what to say. Finally, Ah found mah tongue and Ah said *his joooob?! What did he <u>dooo</u>?! He was Mastah of the Hunt!*

He didn't <u>dooo</u> an'thin'!

At What Point Do We Break

Moonless dark, rain pours as though Noah is expected. The red clay parking lot outside Athens' Ebenezer Baptist Church quickly liquefies. Rev. Martin Luther King Sr. is overdue inside, campaigning for presidential candidate Hubert Humphrey.

October 1968. A half-year after his son's assassination. Months after Washington, Chicago, and 100 other cities riot and burn. A sophomore journalism major, I sit in the back seat of a slumping station wagon interviewing Rev. King for the University of Georgia newspaper.

He has invited me to call him Daddy King, as so many do. After I finish questions about the Vietnam War and racial unrest, I want to ask a personal question. With pastoral patience, he nods acceptance.

Propelled by white righteous naïveté and enraptured by the compassion he exudes, I lean closer and say: *I have a friend, a black girl who is quite promising. She decided at the end of her freshman year she doesn't want to stay at the University. She wants to go North. Doesn't she have a responsibility to stay, to try to improve the situation?*

His shoulders sag slightly and with the baritone resonance of an ageless soul he says *It's according to how much she suffers.* Like a preacher, Daddy King answers my question with a story:

A little niece of mine in Detroit, seven years old, went to school the other day. Teacher was white. A little white boy kept sticking pins in her. She told him to stop. She held up her hand, the teacher told her to put her hand down and study her lesson. She got up and moved. The teacher said, "You go and sit down." The little girl said, "I'm trying to tell you something." And the teacher said, "You get back to your lesson!"

She went back, attempted to sit down, and he kept sticking her. Seven years old. So she got up and walked five blocks home, where her aunt asked why she was home. "Auntie, I couldn't take any more. I just couldn't take any more."

There's a point where we break. How has this individual that you speak of, how much has she had to take?

Overwhelmed by Rev. King's wisdom and singular compassion, I never wrote the newspaper story.

I recalled the interview, though, in June 1974, when I heard his wife had been murdered in their Atlanta church, Ebenezer Baptist. The shooter was a young black man from Kentucky who had intended, that hot summer day, to kill Rev. King. Instead, he shot Alberta King in the side of her head as she played the Lord's Prayer on a newly installed organ to open Sunday service. Rev. King's daughter later said that his wife's murder was even harder for him than his son's, yet he soldiered on, saying the Lord had not given him more than he could take.

Living Inside

The Mist of Mystery

If you pierced the veil
that sometimes skims

scarcely sensed
across your cheek –

a misty presence –
what would you ask of that

or those on the other side:
what is real, what but

a masquerade? Or inquire the truth –
whose hand writes

the poem, whose voice sings
the song? Perhaps you'd lean

scientific, inquiring if all we touch
is illusion, all that endures

invisible. Or probe mysteries pulsing
beyond our sight or sense:

does an old river, weary
of flow, wish rest as meadow pond?

Do oaks decide as one
to leaf, to molt?

Is ocean kin to shore.

To an Artist Turning 18

Tattoos in every crayola color
cover my nephew neck to foot,
appropriate costume for his band

whose music I never hear.
His cloistered art earns him
familial scorn, even on this day

when society crowns him
an adult. At 18, I trusted an aunt –
"the writer" in our family –

with my first poem. She recoiled:
write something happy, she scolded.
I wrote no lines for a quarter century;

once resumed, I hid my poetry
two decades more. Play on, I urge
my nephew, sing your truth;

don't let others silence your music
or shutter your view. If you create for others,
you create falseness. If you create

for yourself, you express truth
however fleeting. Not to express is to die,
not the six-foot-under kind of dead

but the walking-around kind,
far more piteous. Your gift, I say,
was not granted to bring you fawning

from family, regard from friends
or riches from strangers. It was given
so you may unearth your soul.

Five Cents of Satisfaction

It was brown and tan – a pinto,
a horsewoman would say – and I rode
that miniature steed like I'd been born

with dust of the old West thick
in my ginger curls. The reins rested
lightly in my fingers, my five-year-old thighs

held tight against his ribs. My head flew back
as he reared, forward when the hooves
set down. A steel pole in the belly

tethered him to the same spot each week
outside Woolworth's 5&10. A nickel
would wake him and satisfy my lust;

it might as well have been a saddlebag
of silver. A kindly store manager, though doubting
I'd inserted a coin, helped me into the saddle,

slapped that horse on the butt, then left me
to the adventure I'd pined for … and would remember
long after a nickel could finance my fantasies.

Passing Prayer

Each hush to hear
   the sparrow's song
each sigh to see
   the moon full round
each pause to seek
   the rainbow source

What's Inhaled

The act of praying,
not words,
is the soul's supplication.

The silent howl of the heart –
deliverance or steadfastness,
exaltation or anguish –

is the prayer.
Words refract passion
into ether.

So, too, poetry exists
in the experience of living –
sensing transcendence

in a tree, feeling the lips
of a lost lover on an April breeze,
hearing the eternal in a seashell.

Words exhale
what has been inhaled.

By a Stone Already Etched

> It is that absence of being able to envisage
> that you will ever be cheerful again.
> —JK Rowling

Crepe myrtles molt, feathering the grave of summer.
Leaves forsake their limbs. It's fall; you have come

  for me. You lurk behind the dogwood's red tint,
  beneath acorn caps crunching under foot.

    On Halloween, you unveil as ghoul or
    Grim Reaper then don and ditch

      disguise as Thanksgiving morphs
      into Christmas. Earlier and earlier

        each day, you shroud the sun.
        Your harsh breath tumbles me

          inexorably, like sagebrush,
          toward a pit already dug,

            by a stone already
            etched. Carols ring

              afar. The world
              becomes a long,

                silent
                night.

Winter Solstice

So
Often
Lives are
Stilled by the
Thousand tiny cuts
Incurred without notice,
Churned out by daily
Existence in a world without cotton.

The Destiny of Destiny

A minstrel sings into the moonless night,
not knowing if ears hear her song.

Wind scatters seed across chance fields –
maybe fertile, maybe fallow.

A sea turtle quits her eggs in the sand,
never to fathom their fate.

As we are created so we do. Destiny
belongs to Another.

Ode to Late Bloomers

To aspiring athletes
      the ones always picked last,
eager artists
      whose drawings never make the wall,
would-be prom queens
      alone on the dance floor fringe
I say: behold the cherry blossoms
      now flowering on the limb –
      how they color and grace –
while those who bloomed early,
      before the hoary breath of March
      had breathed its last,
hang brown and shriveled at their side.

Stone Still on a Park Bench

Fog settles heavy, wet cotton
into the canyon of my being.
Silence is everywhere.

Despair's Slender Strand

Not today, the flowers need water.
Not today, the dog needs a walk.
Not today, a child is crying.
Not today.

Is It Will to Live

or fear of dying
that sustains this crooked
crippled pine,
half of whose roots
have unclenched the soil?

What of the desiccated oak leaf,
alone and clinging fiercely
long after maples and sycamores
have surrendered
to tomorrow's garden?

What of my desolate mother,
mostly deaf, mostly blind,
mostly bed-ridden, whose mind
has escaped completely
the confines of cognition?

Gold Leaf and Letting Go

I lower myself gingerly onto the fallen trunk,
my aging hip poor padding for an extended sit,
and watch fallen leaves create a moving calico
on the pond's olive surface. Silence surrenders
to a woodpecker's drum and the muffled report
of hunters' guns beyond the ridge. Then both stop;

stillness returns. A beech leaf, gloriously gold,
gently releases from an overhanging limb
and descends with joyous sashay. Its work
is done; its season over. Oh, one day,
may I yield with the grace of a leaf.

Hidden in the Ivy

Ivy vines thick as a thumb
fall victim to frenetic shearing
as I restore the border
to its rightful boundary.

My rusty edger cleaves tendrils
marching across the walk, unmasking
dusky tones of weathered flagstone.
Tears mix with sweat as my hands
make metaphor of gardening within.

Meadow Pond

The river flowing
from the mountain's melting cap
always flows away from
and always flows toward.

It is itself
only in the transition
from the snowmelt of its origin
to the ocean of its destiny.

The pond in the meadow,
fed more from within than without,
is always itself.
It never goes anywhere.

Once a snow-fed river
confident of where I was going,
I am now a meadow pond,
unsure of where I am.

The Redbud

I gaze out the window.
I see you.

Skin flakes from your gnarled trunk.
Pits mar your flesh.

Yet you blossom pink-purple passion
in the first days of spring.

What storms have twisted you?
What balms have blessed?

You are dying. Scars testify
to severed pieces of past
no longer treasured or jewels
lost before their time.

Today a limb thick with years
stands naked but for a few leaves.
When winds cool, they will fall.

You will not. There are springs left
in your soul.

I gaze in the mirror.
I see me.

Time has tattooed itself across
my flesh. My trunk weathers.

Yet my cheeks are blushed
by gloaming; morning lights my eyes.

I have known storm.
I have known balm.

I am dying. I prune what sucks strength
but blooms not and
seek reservoirs to feed
pink-purple promise.

Age sharpens my urgency
to nurture buds too long
neglected, however few.

In every winter is hope of spring.
Pink-purple passion.

Visitation in Leaf Clothing

In the stillness of gloaming
        and silence of deep-forest,
                a lone soul sits
                        on a rotting sycamore stump
                                  heart-hungry.
      A petal-small leaf
            prematurely released
                    tacks slowly southward
                          on currents scented
                                summer-turning-fall.
          The lone soul rises
                  sated.

Toyotas and Transfiguration

Waiting outside the Toyota dealer,
watching a dulcet dance of snowflakes
stage-lit by sodium globes,

I look up
to gunmetal clouds
distinct against a darkening sky.

A drop slipped from one
a minute ago, or maybe five,
drawn down by gravity and fate

              falling
                    falling

morphing
into an ice crystal
that freefell

                  east

  then west
             then south
     drifting
                    drifting
    drifting

and landing as a snowflake on my tongue.
Where did what was
become what is?

Falling

When from the sky the sun too early goes,
and leaves from oak and elm lie on the ground,
the rays that lifted heart and lessened load
take, with their fade, the joy tomorrow sounds;
grim darkness gathers quick and with it woes
forgotten or ignored when light abounds.

Then sorrow comes on every wash and tide:
a sinking scourge of black and sodden doom,
a bitter brine no faith can long abide,
a vinegar that sours hope to gloom.
The Spirit must dive fast if seeks to save
a soul that flails and flounders in the deep
that sinks a foot with every passing wave
and which, in truth, wants nothing but to sleep.

Now Certain

He with sure step comes near the last high tide
and, soul serene, he with his doom abides

for blessed he's been with life most amply churned,
by passions of the heart and head in turn.

He's measured well our tiny, shallow earth,
spinning beneath the sun and stars, its worth

just fool's gold whose sheen diverts the eye
from jeweled treasure he knows certain lies

in that great sea in which we all do swim
and which, truth told, is what is meant by Him.

Ebb Tide

As embers of my coal
turn ash,
the final faint draws near,
lay me
where the ocean meets the sand.

Let salt be
my final kiss, the roil of waves
my requiem.
And when the last flicker of rose
turns gray,
feed me to the fish.

Acknowledgements and Thanks

My thanks to these publications, in which versions of these poems appeared:
    Passager: "Buried Sound," "Ebb Tide."
    Bourgeon: "Statue in the Shallows"
    NOVA Bards 2017: "Horn Concerto in E Flat Is Why I Want to
        Meet Mozart"

I wish to express my great appreciation to Charlotte Matthews, poet and associate professor at the University of Virginia, without whose teaching, coaching and encouragement I would never have seriously addressed writing poetry.

And my bottomless appreciation goes out to my poetry workshop, whose tutelage, reassurance, confidence and friendship not only helped me improve but gave me the courage to keep trying. Thank you, thank you all: Myra Bridgforth, Anne Mugler, Ann Rayburn, Jeremy Taylor and the late Maryhelen Snyder.

Finally, I thank Patricia Goldman for her endless invitations to visit her at Chautauqua, which I finally accepted in 2014. Without that visit, and Charlotte's quick course there, I would never have started on this path.

Photographs of author by Turner G. Bridgforth

About the Author

An author and former journalist, Rebecca King Leet was widely published during her long career in media, public policy and consulting in Washington, DC. She turned to poetry in 2015 as a strategy to support her lifelong tendency to live with intense openness – with the doors wide open – and to use writing as a mean of processing life's moments and memories. She sees the art as means to those ends. The mother of two daughters, she lives in Arlington, VA.

www.ingramcontent.com/pod-product-compliance
Lightning Source LLC
LaVergne TN
LVHW011424080426
835512LV00005B/246